THE GOLDEN YEARS

text: David Sandison

design: Paul Kurzeja

SIENA

197

Welcome to The Golden Years and the events which helped shape 1970 - a memorable year marked by triumph, disaster, delight and grief, with more than enough to pack these pages three times over.

It was a year which saw delight as NASA scientists and a brave crew succeeded in returning the crippled Apollo 13 back to earth when it seemed it must become the first casualty of the space race. It was a year which witnessed triumph for British anti-apartheid protesters when they forced the cancellation of a South African cricket tour. And it was a year of celebration for the people of Brazil as their soccer heroes emerged as World Cup champions.

Palestinian guerrillas found new and explosive ways to pursue their fight with Israel and its Western allies. The IRA stepped up their battle to wrest control of Ulster from the British, and US bombers rained death on the Ho Chi Minh Trail in a vain attempt to stem the flood of Viet Cong forces into South Vietnam.

That tragic war was brought into the American

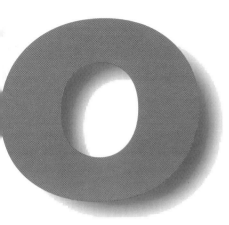

heartland with shocking brutality when four US students died at Kent State University, and with awful clarity when Lt William Calley faced charges of massacring the innocent inhabitants of a South Vietnamese hamlet called My Lai.

France lost a hero when General de Gaulle passed away, and Egypt lost a visionary when President Nasser died of what many said was a broken heart. Millions of pop music fans were broken-hearted too, when Paul McCartney began proceedings to put a final end to The Beatles, but countless thousands celebrated the arrival on TV screens of a series called Monty Python's Flying Circus.

Jagger Fined For Possession, Marianne Acquitted

ARRESTED AND CHARGED with possession of cannabis after police raided their Chelsea home last May, Rolling Stone Mick Jagger and his former lover, the actress-singer Marianne Faithfull, finally found themselves in the dock today. Both denied the charges.

During the hearing, Jagger alleged that the drugs had been planted by a member of the police team led by Det Sgt Robin Constable, the same Drug Squad officer who'd twice raided the homes of Brian Jones, the Rolling Stones guitarist who died last July in a drowning accident. He also alleged that Constable had suggested that a £1,000 'back-hander' would see the matter forgotten.

Since their arrest, the couple - no strangers to world headlines - had flown to Australia where, due to star together in a film about the folk hero Ned Kelly, Marianne had almost died from a drugs overdose. The couple were now almost completely estranged.

Despite his protestations and allegations of attempted bribery, Jagger was found guilty and fined £200 ($500). Marianne was cleared. An official inquiry into Det Sgt Constable's actions would clear him, but he would soon leave the Drug Squad to take up other duties.

Suspension Means Worst News For Best

No extra New Year celebrations for Manchester United's increasingly-wayward star George Best today. The Belfast boy voted European Footballer of the Year in 1968, when his team won the European Cup, was suspended for a month after a Football Association tribunal found him guilty of bringing the game into disrepute.

The 23 year-old striker had begun 1970 pretty much the same way he spent a fair amount of 1969 - butting his head against the football establishment.

Best, who has admitted he likes late nights, lots of drinks and the attention of beautiful blondes, had a number of brushes with authority last year as he missed training sessions, got caught looking the worse for wear by press photographers, and was dropped by Manchester United manager Matt Busby as punishment for other misdemeanours.

Teen Power Dawns As UK Voting Age Reduced

Ultimate proof that the Sixties youth revolution produced more than long hair, flared trousers, ever-louder music and a widespread use of mind-altering substances, came today in Britain when the age of majority was reduced from 21 to 18.

Although opponents of the long and sometimes bitter fight to give teenagers the vote predicted chaos and anarchy if the government introduced the change, its supporters won the day by arguing, successfully, that changes in education and society during the 1960s meant that 18 year olds were every bit as responsible as most of their elders.

With a British general election likely this year, political party chiefs will be busy trying to find ways of attracting the votes of the young millions who'll be entitled to put ticks on ballot papers.

UK TOP 10 SINGLES

1: Two Little Boys
- Rolf Harris

2: Ruby, Don't Take Your Love To Town
- Kenny Rogers & The First Edition

3: All I Have To Do Is Dream
- Bobbie Gentry & Glen Campbell

4: Suspicious Minds
- Elvis Presley

5: Tracy
- The Cuff Links

6: Sugar Sugar
- The Archies

7: Melting Pot
- Blue Mink

8: Good Old Rock 'n' Roll
- The Dave Clark Five

9: Reflections Of My Life
- Marmalade

10: Come And Get It
- Badfinger

DEPARTURES
Died this month
29: Sir Basil Henry Liddell Hart, British historian
31: Slim Harpo, US blues guitarist, singer, songwriter (*I'm A King Bee*, etc)

TO ENSURE BIAFRA'S FR O. WE MUST STEM NIGERIAN AGGRESSION

JANUARY 18

No RIP For Karl, The Workers' Hero

Long a tourist attraction for communists and capitalists alike, the tomb of Karl Marx - the German political philosopher whose seminal treatise Das Kapital provided the world's Communists with a clear blueprint - became the centre of police attention today when it was daubed with Nazi swastikas and damaged in an attempt to blow it up.

Situated at the top of Highgate Cemetery, in north London, Marx's tomb features a huge bust of the revolutionary thinker which stares out over the city which became his home in exile when his political beliefs incurred the wrath of German authorities.

Police would not be able to identify the vandals.

A subscription fund would successfully pay for Marx's resting place to be restored to its former - and lasting - glory.

JANUARY 16

Thousands Die As Hong Kong Flu Strikes

Already a deadly killer in the United States and a number of European countries, the influenza virus known as Hong Kong A2, hit Britain especially hard this month. According to Ministry of Health figures released in London today, 2,850 people were killed by the bug in the week ending January 9. That number, the highest reported from 'flu since 1933, followed the December 19-26 total of 1,421 fatalities and the 2,400 reported during the following week.

Ministry experts suggested that the worst might be over, however. A breakdown of figures indicated Hong Kong Flu was waning in the south, with most of the recent cases confined to north-west England.

Spanish Princess Tells Of Biafran Horror

REPORTS OF WIDESCALE STARVATION, and murder, looting and rape by government troops in Biafra - the rebel East Nigerian province whose leaders surrendered last week to end almost two years of civil war - were confirmed today by the Spanish Princess, Cecile de Bourbon-Parma, who fled Biafra just before the surrender.

'There was massacre all the way as the federal troops advanced', she told journalists. 'The people were separated into three groups - men, women and children. The men were all killed.'

The Princess also alleged that many women were raped before being killed, but could not confirm the fate of the children she'd seen rounded up. Her first-hand account matches those of Western journalists allowed to visit the region since Biafran leader General Odumegwa Ojukwu capitulated and escaped to the Ivory Coast.

During the conflict, which was sparked by the Ibo tribe's decision to take its homeland out of the Nigerian political system, Britain supported the federal government while France backed the Biafrans. The breakaway region became the site of privation and starvation as food and medical supplies were blockaded, while continued British arms supplies to the forces of Nigeria's President, General Gowon, meant Ojukwu's defeat was inevitable.

Late, But Welcome - PanAm's First

Despite last-minute technical hitches which forced engineers to change one of its engines before it could leave New York's JFK Airport, Pan American Airways' first Boeing 747 - the huge passenger jet nicknamed 'The Jumbo' - touched down at London's Heathrow Airport today to inaugurate a new era in world travel.

It may have been three hours late, and bad weather may have forced PanAm to cancel a scheduled onward flight to Frankfurt, Germany, but the graceful giant received an excited welcome from thousands of plane-spotters who packed Heathrow terraces and airport perimeter roads to catch their first glimpse of the future.

Twice as big as the Boeing 707 it was destined to replace, the Jumbo weighed in at 350 tons, with a passenger capacity of 362. Its extra-large hold also created problems for Heathrow baggage handlers, and a lot of luggage went astray in the crush.

Police Clash With Anti-Vietnam Protesters

A torchlit peace procession of 2,000 people trying to deliver a petition condemning Prime Minister Harold Wilson's decision to visit Washington while the United States is still embroiled in the Vietnam War, turned to violence tonight as police blocked access to Downing Street. A number of officers - including senior policemen - were injured as marchers began using placards as batons. Those not used this way became the fuel for bonfires the protesters built on Parliament Square, the garden area opposite the House of Commons.

Russell, Eternal Rebel Philosopher, Dies

BERTRAND RUSSELL, (pictured) the British philosopher, mathematician, nuclear disarmament rebel and serial lover, died today at the age of 97.

A radical thinker who re-defined mathematics by arguing that it could be entirely deduced from logic, Russell was imprisoned and dismissed from his first Cambridge University fellowship because of his opposition to World War I, married four times, enjoyed numerous affairs, was barred from lecturing in the United States during the 1940s because of his public views on sexual libertarianism, won the Nobel Prize for Literature in 1950, helped found the Campaign for Nuclear Disarmament and served a prison term for his anti-nuclear beliefs at the age of 88.

Russell's life was a full one. According to the preface of his autobiography, published in 1993, it was a life governed by three passions: '...the longing for love, the search for knowledge and unbearable pity for the sufferings of mankind.'

Even his harshest critics agreed that Russell's *A History Of Western Philosophy,* the work which won him that Nobel Prize, was a masterpiece. The man himself? He was a one-off.

FEBRUARY 9

Equal Pay Bill Passes Second Reading Hurdle

The British government's Bill to give women the same pay as men came closer to becoming law today when it was passed unopposed in its second reading in the House of Commons.

Aimed at achieving a same-job-same-salary goal by 1976, the Bill came in for only the mildest of opposition when one Conservative back-bencher suggested that many women would lose their jobs if employers had to pay them a higher rate.

Employment Secretary Barbara Castle, on the other hand, suggested that the Bill would lead to greater efficiency and a better use of labour. However, she warned that women could, and still would, demand to keep existing special privileges, such as maternity leave with the right to return to work in the same job.

FEBRUARY 16

Ellis Counted Out, Frazier New Heavyweight Champ

Joe Frazier emerged as the new undisputed heavyweight champion of the world tonight at New York's Madison Square Garden when he knocked out the WBA title-holder, Jimmy Ellis, in the fourth round of a contest which also helped confirm his fearsome reputation as a ferocious fighter.

Aged 26, Frazier was born the seventh son of a poor South Carolina farmer, moved to Philadelphia to take work in an abattoir and became a highly-rated amateur boxer.

Picked to represent the United States in the 1964 Tokyo Olympics, he returned with a gold medal and a burning ambition to turn pro.

Unbeaten since, Frazier's victory tonight - and his claim to being the best - would be accepted by everyone except supporters of Muhammad Ali, stripped of his title in 1967 for refusing, as a newly-converted Muslim, to serve in Vietnam. A fight between Frazier and Ali just had to be on the cards...

FEBRUARY 11

Sellers And Starr Slammed For 'Magic' Movie

Critics were universally scathing in their opinions of *The Magic Christian*, the Peter Sellers-Ringo Starr film which premièred in New York tonight. Despite a script which included surreal material by *Monty Python* stars John Cleese and Graham Chapman, the general view was that the movie was an unfunny mess.

Based on a novel by Terry Southern (who, with Sellers and director Joseph McGrath, also wrote the main screenplay), it told how the world's wealthiest man (Sellers) and his simpleton protégé (Starr) set out to prove that people will do anything - no matter how stupid, tasteless or gross - for money.

About the only thing people liked about *The Magic Christian* was the music soundtrack supplied by Liverpool group Badfinger. *Come And Get It,* a song written and produced by Paul McCartney, became an international hit this month.

ARRIVALS
Born this month:
27: Kent Desormeaux, US champion jockey

DEPARTURES
Died this month:
2: Bertrand Arthur William Russell, Third Earl Russell, British philosopher, mathematician *(see main story)*
11: Henry Mayo Bateman, British cartoonist
13: Hirsch Jacobs, leading US racehorse trainer 1924-1960
14: Herbert Strudwick, English wicket-keeper (Surrey 1902-1927)
15: Air Chief Marshal Hugh Caswall Tremenheere Dowding, 1st Baron Dowding, British WWII Air Force commander
25: Mark Rothko, US artist

FEBRUARY 21

Rave Reviews Mean Mary's Gonna Make It!

Broadcast for the first time across the United States this month, The *Mary Tyler Moore Show* (pictured) proved a huge hit with critics and viewers alike, with praise shared equally by its star (still America's sweetheart, thanks to constant re-runs of the sixties hit series *The Dick Van Dyke Show*) and the excellent cast assembled round her. They included Valerie Harper, who'd go on to star in a hit series based on her character (*Rhoda*), Cloris Leachman, whose Phyllis would also spin off to great success, and Ed Asner (pictured), whose gruff TV station newsroom boss *Lou Grant* would provide him with gainful employment between 1977 and 1982. As the show's theme song concluded, while our Mary headed for the uncertainties of a move to The Big City: 'You're gonna make it after all!'

More than anything, though, *The Mary Tyler Moore Show* enabled the dynamic Miss Moore to begin building her own MTM-TV production company which would create future classics like *Lou Grant* and the 1980s medical drama *St Elsewhere*.

German Court Rules Anna Is Not Anastasia

A GERMAN COURT TODAY dashed the hopes of Anna Anderson, a former lady's maid, in her latest attempt to prove that she was, in fact, Anastasia, the only surviving daughter of Czar Nicholas II, the last Emperor of Russia. It rejected her claim that she had managed to avoid being killed by Bolsheviks who slaughtered the Russian royal family in 1918 to end the Romanoff empire.

The woman who had fought to establish her claim to the untold millions lying in Western bank vaults for almost 50 years was clearly disappointed with the verdict, but swore she would continue the fight to prove her identity. Certainly, her apparently intimate knowledge of events leading up to the massacre of Czar Nicholas, his wife Alexandra and their children at Ekaterinburg during the turmoil and confusion of the Russian revolution, impressed many. Apparently, it was not enough to sway the jury.

Anna/Anastasia's story had long fascinated conspiracy theorists, and had led to her version of events being told in the 1956 movie Anastasia. While it had won Ingrid Bergman an Oscar, it didn't win today's plaintiff the verdict she most wanted - recognition of her real identity.

Prince Charles To Join Navy

Prince Charles will join the British Navy when he completes his studies at Cambridge University, it was confirmed in a statement released by Buckingham Palace today.

The announcement ended months of speculation about the Prince's future. It is traditional for future British monarchs to serve in one of the services. However, Prince Charles is the first heir to the throne to undertake a university degree course, and that break with tradition led some commentators to suggest that he may choose to pursue another career.

While big-wigs in the army and air force will doubtless be disappointed Prince Charles has elected to join the navy, few Palace-watchers were surprised. His father, the Duke of Edinburgh, was a navy man before he met Princess - now Queen - Elizabeth. And Prince Philip is known to be a man used to having his say, and his way.

UK Musicians Threaten Albert Hall Ban

Britain's Musicians Union threatened to blacklist London's prestigious Royal Albert Hall this month after the venue's management refused to play host to a charity event planned for March. Intended to raise funds for the National Council for Civil Liberties and Release, the organization which aids drugs offenders, the show was to have featured John Lennon, The Who, King Crimson and The Incredible String Band. The management's decision followed its controversial banning of a Rolling Stones concert last December. As the hall normally presents some 40 rock concerts each year, there was suspicion that the vetoes were politically inspired. More worrying than a rock band blacklist, a Musicians Union ban would jeopardize the classical events which more usually grace the hall - including the annual month-long Promenade Concerts season.

Nixon Steps Up Bombing As Cambodians Oust Sihanouk

PRESIDENT RICHARD NIXON today ordered General Creighton Abrams, US Commander in Vietnam, to step up the bombing of North Vietnamese forces moving through eastern Laos on what has become known as 'the Ho Chi Minh Trail'.

US bombing of the trail - one of North Vietnam's principal supply routes to communist troops who have begun mounting major assaults on its neighbour to the west - had already proved controversial. More than 200 sorties by B52 bombers were known to be taking place already, so the increase represented a massive attack plan bound to provide America's anti-Vietnam War movement with further ammunition.

President Nixon's move was inevitable. The fall of Laos would have severe implications for the security of Thailand and, of course, for US forces in Vietnam.

Viet Cong troops were also reported active in Cambodia, and on March 18 Cambodian right-wingers took advantage of the absence of Prince Sihanouk - their Head of State, in Moscow for talks with Russian Prime Minister Kosygin - to seize power.

Although the prince was attempting to persuade Kosygin to pressure North Vietnam to pull an estimated 50,000 troops out of Cambodia, the new junta was too impatient, as were the mobs who'd stormed and sacked North Vietnamese and Viet Cong missions in the Cambodian capital, Phnom Penh.

On March 30, Cambodia's Prime Minister, Lon Nol, would ask for US arms to help repel their incursions.

1: Wand'rin Star
- Lee Marvin
2: Bridge Over Troubled Water
- Simon & Garfunkel
3: I Want You Back
- The Jackson Five
4: Let It Be
- The Beatles
5: Let's Work Together
- Canned Heat
6: Instant Karma
- John Lennon, Yoko Ono & The Plastic Ono Band
7: That Same Old Feeling
- Pickettywitch
8: Years May Come, Years May Go
- Herman's Hermits
9: Love Grows (Where My Rosemary Goes)
- Edison Lighthouse
10: Na Na Hey Hey Kiss Him Goodbye
- Steam

MARCH 16

Pop World Mourns Death Of Tumour Victim Tammi

Sadness in the pop music world today as it learned that Tammi Terrell, the 24 year old singer most famous for her hit duets with Marvin Gaye, had died after undergoing the latest of a series of operations on the brain tumour which ended her career two and a half years ago.

A former psychology and pre-med student at the University of Pennsylvania, Tammi - real name Tammy Montgomery - was discovered and signed by the legendary Tamla Motown company in 1965. She enjoyed a few hits on her own, but her teaming with Gaye resulted in even greater success with songs such as *Ain't Nothing Like The Real Thing, You're All I Need To Get By, Your Precious Love* and *Ain't No Mountain High Enough.*

In 1967 Tammi collapsed on-stage in Virginia, Marvin Gaye carrying her off into the wings. Originally diagnosed as suffering from exhaustion, further tests revealed that Tammi in fact had a brain tumour which would prove fatal, despite a series of operations at Philadelphia's Graduate Hospital.

Makarios Escapes Assassination Attack

MARCH 8

Archbishop Makarios, the Greek Cypriot leader who has been the island's President since 1960, escaped death today when his helicopter was riddled with machine gun fire as it took off from the grounds of the presidential palace in Nicosia.

The would-be assassins had set up their weapon on the roof of a nearby school, from where they had an unobstructed view of the palace. While their intended target was not injured, his pilot was hit three times in the stomach. Despite this, he managed to land safely.

Police arrested three men, all of whom were said to be linked to the banned National Front movement, a terrorist organization which seeks Enosis, union with Greece.

MARCH 16

New Bible Is Runaway Best-Seller

Unprecedented scenes in British bookstores today as one million copies of the New English Bible were purchased on its publication. A modern language revision of the traditional St. James version, its overwhelming success took the publishing world by surprise.

Responding to the rush, the Oxford and Cambridge University Presses ordered an immediate re-printing of 20,000 copies a week, with greatest priority being given to the edition which includes the Apocrypha, the additional Old Testament text not included in the Hebrew Bible and still the subject of scholarly controversy.

MARCH 24

Cooper Regains UK Heavyweight Crown

Controversially barred from trying to win the WBA version of the world heavyweight title from US champion Jimmy Ellis last year because the British Boxing Board of Control did not recognize the WBA, Henry Cooper returned from his self-imposed retirement as British and Empire champion when he fought Jack Bodell (pictured), the man who'd taken that title during his absence. To the obvious delight of a partisan London audience, Cooper reclaimed the crown. He did so knowing that if he was to be given another shot at the world championship, it would not be against Ellis. He'd been knocked out by Joe Frazier last month - something Cooper had been confident he could have done, given the chance.

MARCH 21

Czech Communists Suspend Dubček

The Czechoslovak Communist Party drove a final nail into the political coffin of former national leader Alexander Dubček today when it suspended his membership, thereby effectively cutting him off from meaningful employment and public office.

The man who introduced the sweeping reforms of 'The Prague Spring' to liberalize Czech society in 1968, but was ousted in that August when Russian and Warsaw Pact troops moved in to re-impose hard-line authority, had been allowed to stay on as Speaker of the Federal Assembly.

That role has also been taken from Dubček, and there are reports he is to be banished to Bratislava.

MARCH 29

British Troops Seal Off Bogside

British military commanders in Londonderry today ordered the Catholic Bogside area to be sealed off after troops came under attack from stone-throwing rioters.

The disturbances were said to be the worst for some time, and certainly the worst since December when the militant Ulster civil rights MP, Bernadette Devlin, was sentenced to six months imprisonment for her part in last August's riots when troops were first sent to Ulster to protect the Catholic community from growing Protestant attacks.

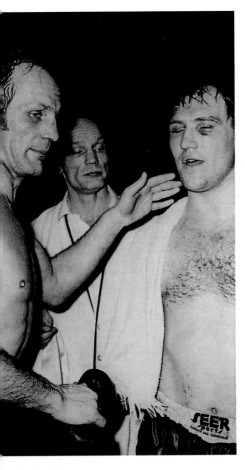

Thalidomide Victims Claim First Victory In High Court

THE FAMILIES AND LAWYERS of 18 British children born with severe defects in the late 1950s and early 1960s today began celebrating an historic victory in their High Court action against the giant Distillers (Biochemicals) Company, British licensees of thalidomide, the German-made morning sickness drug taken during pregnancy by all the mothers involved in the case.

The families - who had successfully argued that Distillers promoted and sold thalidomide in Britain despite knowing that reports of serious side-effects were being investigated in Germany - were awarded damages totalling £370,000 ($750,000), which included reparation for distress and parents' loss of earnings.

That sum is to be allocated to individual children in proportion to the severity of their disabilities. The worst cases - five children born with 'flipper' arms - would receive £28,000 (almost $60,000) each. Today's result is sure to act as an invaluable precedent for another 28 British families who have lawsuits awaiting trial, and lawyers representing victims in Germany.

VICTORY FOR PATTON AS TANKS MEET HANKIES IN OSCARS BATTLE

Knowing just how much America loves its war heroes (especially at a time when it was transparently obvious that the Vietnam War was a lost cause and the My Lai massacre was proving how shamefully some of its people were fighting in that conflict), the Best Film Oscar won by *Patton,* and the Best Actor award presented to George C Scott for his portrayal of the General who bucked the system and beat superior German forces in World War II, ought to have been a safe bet in this year's Academy Awards.

So it proved, even though *Patton* did face stiff competition for Best Picture in the form of the runaway cult hit *Five Easy Pieces*, the Korean War tragi-comedy *M*A*S*H,* the silly but very succesful *Airport* and the four-hankie weepy *Love Story.*

The competition for Best Director was even more wide open, with Hollywood's favourite Italian, Federico Fellini, nominated for *Fellini Satyricon,* Robert Altman for

M*A*S*H, Ken Russell for *Women In Love,* Arthur Hiller for *Love Story* and Franklin J Schnaffner, for *Patton.* Schnaffer won to give his film the Big Three awards.

With no females at all featuring in that, the Best Actress category seemed to give Ali McGraw's doomed *Love Story* heroine an automatic hot-favourite status in the betting. However, she found herself up against an excellent Jane Alexander in the boxing melodrama *The Great White Hope,* an especially on-form Sarah Miles in *Ryan's Daughter,* a powerful Carrie Snodgrass in *Diary Of A Mad Housewife* - and a flawless Glenda Jackson in *Women In Love.* It was Jackson who got it.

Another Brit, veteran John Mills, won a well-deserved Supporting Actor award for his village idiot in *Ryan's Daughter,* while the equally venerable Helen Hayes was presented with the Supporting Actress trophy for *Airport.*

Only Nino Navarese's costume design won something for *Cromwell,* the big budget flop of the year which had fervent Irish nationalist Richard Harris playing Oliver

Cromwell, the Englishman who first made a blood sport out of England's treatment of the Irish people.

The Feature Documentary prize was won by the excellent footage put together during the three days of peace, love, drugs and mud that had been the 1969 festival at *Woodstock,* while the gung-ho achievements of *Patton* were quietly counter-balanced by the Oscar for Short Documentary awarded to *Interviews With My Lai Veterans.*

Two Honorary Oscars were awarded - one to silent screen goddess Lillian Gish, the other to Hollywood bad boy Orson Welles. He, the audience and watching millions were told, could not accept his award in person because he was filming in Spain. To prove it, Welles appeared on film to thank the Academy for this signal honour. John Huston accepted Orson's Oscar, left the awards ceremony, drove across Los Angeles, and handed the statuette to his friend while they enjoyed a celebratory supper!

APRIL

Unlucky Apollo 13 Limps Safely Home

WITH THE WORLD watching anxiously, the 90-hour cliff-hanger drama of *Apollo 13* ended triumphantly today when the crippled moon craft's capsule splashed down in the Pacific, its three man crew - James Lovell, Fred Haise and John Swigert - reported safe and well.

The *Apollo 13* mission appeared doomed when an explosion ripped through the service module as the craft entered space and began its intended journey to the moon. With vital air and life support systems running low, the engine crippled and the crew unable to turn back, they were forced to take refuge in the tiny lunar module for most of their unplanned journey around the moon.

As NASA scientists worked tirelessly to help *Apollo 13* return to earth, no-one was in any doubt that the lives of those on board hung by a thread. As the countdown to re-entry began, the three heroes crawled back into the main spacecraft and successfully steered her home to universal relief and not a few tears.

Troops 'Will Shoot' Ulster Petrol Bombers

The British Army today confirmed a new 'get tough' policy against Ulster rioters who throw petrol bombs, saying that any who ignore warnings from officers at the scene would be 'liable to be shot dead in the street' if they continued.

Confirmation came from General Sir Ian Freeland, General Officer Commanding the 6,000 troops now based in Northern Ireland, as he announced that they were to be reinforced by a further 500 men.

Sir Ian said that there were 'sinister people' behind the teenagers who'd caused the most recent outbreaks of street violence. Commentators were quick to assume that he meant the IRA was masterminding the civil unrest.

Arab Children Killed By Israeli Jets

The ever-present tension between Israel and its Arab neighbours exploded this month into what reporters described as 'the most serious fighting since the 1967 Six Day War' when Israeli and Syrian troops went into battle on April 2.

World opinion was focused into outrage six days later when it was learned that at least 30 Arab children had been killed when Israeli jet bombers attacked the village of Bahr al Bakar.

Towards the end of the month, Israeli forces near the northern border with Lebanon came under repeated attacks from Palestinian terrorists. Its patience finally exhausted, the Israeli Government would order a major offensive into southern Lebanon on May 11, with suspected PLO bases its stated targets. At least 50 Arabs would be reported killed in the 32-hour raid.

Simon and Garfunkel: No 1 with Bridge Over Troubled Water

APRIL 30

Defiant Nixon Orders US Into Cambodia

President Nixon made a surprise television address to the American people tonight, telling them that he had ordered US combat troops to attack communist forces based in Cambodia. Clearly aware that his decision was likely to create controversy and increased protests, he defiantly told his audience: 'I would rather be a one-term President than a two-term President at the cost of seeing America become a second-rate power and accept the first defeat in its history.'

Defending his move, Mr Nixon stressed that it should not be viewed as an invasion of Cambodia. The areas selected for attack by US and South Vietnamese troops were occupied by North Vietnamese forces which the Cambodian people themselves had been trying to evict.

The principal target was the headquarters for the entire Communist military operation in South Vietnam, a command centre which the President said had been occupied by the North Vietnamese and Viet Cong for years 'in blatant violation of Cambodia's neutrality.'

Unusually frank, Mr Nixon prefaced his 'one-term President' remarks by admitting that senior Republican Party members had warned him the Cambodian invasion could end his chances of re-election in November. 'No-one', he said 'is more aware than I am of the political consequences.'

ARRIVALS

Born this month:
16: Gabriella Sabatini, Argentinian tennis star
18: Heiki Friedrich, East German freestyle swimming star - former European, World and Olympic champion
29: Andre Agassi, US tennis ace

DEPARTURES

Died this month:
11: John (Henry) O'Hara, US novelist, screenwriter (*Pal Joey, Butterfield 8*)
25: Otis Spann, US blues pianist, long-time accompanist of his half-brother, Muddy Waters
27: Earl Hooker, US blues slide guitarist
28: Ed (Edward James) Begley, US Oscar-winning film and stage actor (*Sweet Bird Of Youth, 12 Angry Men, Billion Dollar Brain*, etc)

APRIL 9

McCartney Solo LP Means The Beatles' Dream Is Over

PAUL McCARTNEY ENDED MONTHS of rumour and speculation of a growing rift between him and the other members of The Beatles today when he discussed the imminent release of his first solo LP, simply titled *McCartney* and said he did not intend to write songs with John Lennon any more.

Although The Beatles' new album, *Let It Be,* was scheduled for release in May and the title track had already given The Fab Four their twenty-third consecutive Top 10 hit, it was widely understood it had been recorded in an increasingly frosty atmosphere, with McCartney unhappy about the constant presence and growing influence of John Lennon's wife, the Japanese artist Yoko Ono. He was also known to be furious with his erstwhile partners' decision to appoint American lawyer Allen Klein as their manager.

He was not the first of The Fab Four to record and release material on his own. John Lennon and Yoko Ono had already scored big hits with *Give Peace A Chance, Cold Turkey* and *Instant Karma,* while drummer Ringo Starr had released his own solo album *Sentimental Journey* a week or two earlier.

Although it would take more than three years of increasingly acrimonious and vicious legal wrangling before The Beatles would cease to exist legally, Paul McCartney's decision to go to law early next year effectively meant that the most influential and successful musical team of the sixties was no more. The dream was well and truly over.

APRIL 29

Chelsea Beat Leeds In Replayed Cup Final

Chelsea FC became England's 1970 FA Cup champions today at Wembley Stadium when they beat Leeds United in a replay which, like their first encounter on April 11, had to go to an extra half-hour when the scheduled 90-minute game ended with the two teams tied.

On that first occasion, the extra 30 minutes saw them level at 2-2. Today's game ended 1-1 at the final whistle, but a second Chelsea goal in extra time was enough to settle things. After four hours of exhausting and - for fans of both sides - nerve-racking action, it was Chelsea who crawled up the steps to take possession of the trophy and their hard-earned winners' medals.

APRIL 7

Oscar For Duke Wayne's True Grit

A staggering 42 years after making his first screen appearance, Hollywood superstar John Wayne finally won his industry's most treasured prize - a Best Actor Oscar - at this year's Academy Awards ceremony.

Known to his friends as 'Duke', the grizzled 63 year old star won his Oscar for his portrayal of a grizzled sixty-something marshal in the Western *True Grit* - a role he modestly described as 'the easiest of my career.'

That career had seen some of Wayne's best performances completely overlooked as far as awards were concerned, most notably *Stagecoach* in 1939, *The Quiet Man* in 1952 *The Searchers* in 1956 and the 1960 epic *The Alamo*, which he produced and directed, as well as starred in as the frontier hero Davy Crockett.

APRIL 29

Judge Doubts Kennedy Testimony

Although returning a verdict of accidental death, the judge presiding at the inquest of Mary Jo Kopechne - the young political aide found drowned in the back seat of a car Senator Edward Kennedy admitted he'd been driving when it crashed off a bridge on Chappaquiddick Island in New England last July - said that he doubted the truth of the Senator's evidence.

Miss Kopechne and another young woman had been guests at a party in the house of Joseph Gargan, Senator Kennedy's cousin. According to the Senator, he took a wrong turning by mistake and, although he tried to rescue the 27 year old as the car filled with water, he was unsuccessful.

Mystery still surrounds the eight hours known to have elapsed between the accident and Senator Kennedy reporting it to local police.

MAY 4

Student Protesters Killed In Kent State Tragedy

THE VIETNAM WAR CLAIMED its first fatalities in the American heartland today when National Guard soldiers opened fire on students calling for a US pull-out. Four unarmed protesters were killed, and many others wounded, in the incident at Ohio's Kent State University (pictured), which only served to increase opposition to President Nixon's decision to extend US involvement into Cambodia.

While world attention was focused on events in Ohio, two black students were also shot dead during a demonstration at Jackson State University, in Mississippi.

The tragedy began three days ago, when Ohio State National Guard troops were called to the university to break up increasingly rowdy demonstrations. While they succeeded, using tear gas and bayonets, today's protest by 500 students ended in death when the soldiers believed they were being fired at by a sniper hiding on a campus rooftop and began their disastrous response.

President Nixon's response was to call on all American universities - teachers, students and administrators alike - to support the right of peaceful dissent. Although he said

he deplored the students' deaths, Nixon enraged many by adding: 'When dissent turns to violence it invites tragedy.'

Besides the nationwide furore caused by the Kent State shootings, the President also faced a constitutional crisis. Senator George McGovern, a Democrat member of the Foreign Relations Committee, began moves to cut off money for Vietnam War appropriations.

A growing number of leading politicians of both parties were reported to be troubled by Nixon's decision to by-pass Congress in his expansion of the war. On May 5 he would be forced to promise a US withdrawal from Cambodia 'in three to seven weeks.'

MCC Calls Off South African Tour

Confronted by increased opposition to the planned tour by a South African team, the MCC - the official English cricket authority - was forced to admit defeat today and announce that it had been cancelled, only a week before the tourists were due to arrive in London.

Although the international cricket body, the Test and County Cricket Board, had voiced its determination for the tour to go ahead, the publicly-stated opposition of the Home Secretary, James Callaghan, undoubtedly played its part in helping the MCC decide to call it off.

Today's announcement also signalled a victory for Peter Hain, the South African-born anti-apartheid campaigner. Leader and vocal spokesman of the 'Stop the '70 Tour' movement, he had promised all-out disruption of games.

UK Government Bails Out Rolls-Royce

Already forced to inject £47 million ($100m) to ensure the delivery of new RB211 jet engines ordered for the Lockheed *Tri-Star* and BAC *One-Eleven* passenger planes, the British government today loaned manufacturers Rolls-Royce a further £20 million.

Crippled by the vast cost of developing the RB211, Rolls-Royce had appealed for further help to save the project.

It came at a humiliating cost to the ailing company - a representative of the government's Industrial Reorganisation Corporation will be appointed to the Rolls-Royce board, and he will monitor allocation of the loan very closely.

My Lai Journalist Wins Pulitzer Prize

Seymour Hersh, the American journalist who broke the scandal of the 1968 My Lai Massacre in the *New York Times* last November, was today awarded the prestigious Pulitzer Prize for international reporting.

Hersh's story exposed the full horror of events in the tiny Vietnamese village, when US soldiers in a patrol searching for Viet Cong guerrillas slaughtered 567 men, women and children.

Following an urgent Army inquiry, Lt William Calley, the patrol leader, was charged with the murder of at least 109 of the innocent villagers. Both he and his commanding officer, Capt Ernest Medina, are to face a court martial shortly.

UK TOP 10 SINGLES

1: Back Home
- The England World Cup Squad

2: Spirit In The Sky
- Norman Greenbaum

3: House Of The Rising Sun
- Frijid Pink

4: All Kinds Of Everything
- Dana

5: Daughter Of Darkness
- Tom Jones

6: Question
- The Moody Blues

7: Yellow River
- Christie

8: Bridge Over Troubled Water
- Simon & Garfunkel

9: Travellin' Band
- Creedence Clearwater Revival

10: Can't Help Falling In Love
- Andy Williams

DEPARTURES
Died this month:
14: Sir William Dobell, Australian painter
17: Nigel Martin Balchin, UK novelist, screenwriter *(Mine Own Executioner, Suspect, etc)*
27: Ezzard Charles, US heavyweight boxer - World Champion 1949-1951

MAY 28

Bobby Moore Accused Of Bracelet Theft

ENGLAND FOOTBALL CAPTAIN BOBBY MOORE rejoined his team-mates in Mexico today after spending two days in police custody in Bogotá, capital of Colombia, accused of stealing a gold bracelet from an hotel jewellery shop.

The 29 year old midfield maestro, who had consistently and vehemently denied the charges made by the shop's manager, told waiting pressmen, 'I'm very happy to be a free man once more, and pleased the accusations have been proved to be unfounded.'

That last point wasn't strictly true. Moore - in South America to lead the reigning World Cup champions in defence of the title they won at Wembley Stadium in 1966 - had only been released provisionally, while police continued their enquiries. He had to report regularly to Colombian officials in Mexico, and had agreed to present himself at their London embassy in 30 days to hear the result of the case.

Although the judge who ordered Moore's release had wished him well, saying that he hoped he would score 'many goals', the captain's arrest had severely disrupted England's preparations for the World Cup tournament.

Playing all their first round games in Guadalajara, they beat Romania 1-0 on June 2, were beaten 1-0 by eventual champions Brazil five days later, but won a place in the knock-out quarter finals by defeating Czechoslovakia 1-0. On June 14, England's participation in the 1970 World Cup would end when Germany overcame a 2-0 deficit to beat them 3-2.

And the charges against Bobby Moore? They were dropped, and his name was cleared.

(See Sports pages for full World Cup report)

MAY 28

Irish Ex-Ministers Charged With Gun-Running

The recent discovery and seizure of an arms cache at Dublin Airport became a potential political bombshell today when two former cabinet members - ex-Finance Minister Charles Haughey and Neil Blaney, one-time Minister of Agriculture - appeared in a Dublin court, charged with complicity in the haul.

Both men denied the charges and were released on bail to face a huge scrum outside the court as news media, political supporters and curious onlookers tried to catch a quote, a picture or a glimpse of them and four others who were also charged.

Haughey and Blaney had been dismissed by Irish Prime Minister Jack Lynch once he was told they had been named in security service reports of gun-running to Republican terrorists in Ulster. Blaney would be cleared of the charges against him in July, but it would not be until October that Haughey and the others would finally come to trial.

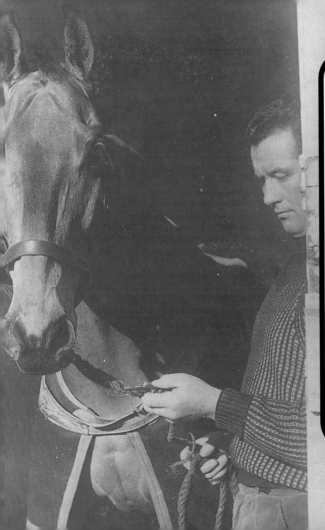

Arkle, The Punters' Favourite, Dies

British and Irish followers of 'the sport of kings' were in mourning today when it was announced that *Arkle,* arguably the greatest steeplechaser of all time, had died in Ireland, aged 13.

Winner of the Cheltenham Gold Cup in 1964, 1965 and 1966, *Arkle* also won the Irish Grand National in 1964, the Whitbread Gold Cup and King George VI Chase in 1965, the Hennessy Gold Cup in 1964 and 1965, and the Leopardstown Chase in 1964 and 1966.

Although *Arkle* lost the first of his famous battles with *Mill House* when he slipped on landing at the final ditch in the 1963 Hennessy, he emerged victor in their 1964 Cheltenham clash, and was never bested by *Mill House* again. Winner of a then-record £78,824 prize money, *Arkle* was forced to retire when he broke a pedal bone in the 1966 King George VI Chase.

JUNE

JUNE 26

Ulster Police 'Kidnap' MP Bernadette As Appeal Fails

Ulster police triggered a violent demonstration in Londonderry tonight when they arrested Bernadette Devlin MP at a road block as she tried to reach a meeting of 1,000 supporters. Instead, she found herself being driven to prison, to start a six-month sentence for incitement to riot - a jail term the High Court had earlier ruled she could not take on appeal to the House of Lords.

Associates of the 23 year old independent MP for Mid-Ulster claimed Devlin intended to surrender to the police later, under the terms of an agreement she had made with the authorities.

News of the police 'kidnap' of the Catholic civil rights activist angered the Bogside crowd, and British troops were only able to restore order when they used canisters of CS gas to disperse youths hurling petrol bombs and stones. More than 20 soldiers were injured.

JUNE 4

Nijinsky And Lester Dance To Derby Victory

Already a firm favourite with the racing public, thanks to his startling run of seven consecutive wins since his début as a two year-old last year, the brilliant colt Nijinsky gave champion jockey Lester Piggott one of the smoothest rides of his career at Epsom Racecourse today when he won The Derby classic in the fastest time since 1936.

Today's victory would prove to be only one-third of an historic treble - Nijinsky would be the first horse for 35 years to win the British Triple Crown of The 2000 Guineas, Derby and St Leger, while also claiming the Irish Derby and the King George VI and Queen Elizabeth Stakes.

Canadian bred and trained by Richard O'Brien in Ireland, Nijinsky would prove victorious in 11 of the 13 races he'd enter, winning £282,223 before being retired to Kentucky for stud duties. He proved pretty good at those, too!

Heath Is New PM As Tories Win Surprise Election

INVITED BY PRIME MINISTER Harold Wilson to give him and the Labour Party up to another five years as the British government, the electorate took Mr Wilson, all opinion poll companies and most political commentators by surprise today when - against all expectations - it voted to give the job to the Conservative Party, so making Edward Heath the new occupant of 10 Downing Street, the official residence of the Prime Minister.

As Mr Heath, a bachelor, international yachtsman, noted musician and conductor, waved to a cheering crowd and promised 'strong and honest government', a bewildered Labour Party leadership began an immediate inquest on their defeat. Made complacent by their apparent supremacy in the polls, they had to face the reality of a House of Commons which would have 330 Conservative MPs, while Labour could only muster 287, with the Liberals winning six seats and other parties taking seven.

Labour's most notable casualty was former Foreign Secretary George Brown, who lost his Belper, Derbyshire, seat to Conservative Geoffrey Stewart-Smith.

Mr Wilson had waged a presidential-style campaign, attempting to sell himself as a calm statesman who'd steered Britain back to prosperity. It appeared Britain preferred to believe Mr Heath, who depicted Labour as straw men trampled by greedy trade union leaders whose pay demands had created only more rising prices and whose orders to strike had led to a widespread sense of insecurity.

On June 21, the Prime Minister announced the first major appointments to his Cabinet team. Former PM Sir Alec Douglas-Home became Foreign Secretary, Reginald Maudling was named as Home Secretary, and Iain Macleod was made Chancellor of the Exchequer.

UK TOP 10 SINGLES

1: Yellow River
- Christie

2: In The Summertime
- Mungo Jerry

3: Groovin' With Mr Bloe
- Mr Bloe

4: Honey Come Back
- Glen Campbell

5: Back Home
- The England World Cup Squad

6: Cottonfields
- The Beach Boys

7: Everything Is Beautiful
- Ray Stevens

8: Question
- The Moody Blues

9: Up The Ladder To The Roof
- The Supremes

10: Sally
- Gerry Monroe

Born this month:
26: Marina Loback, Russian Olympic rhythmic gymnastics champion

DEPARTURES

Died this month:
1: Bruce McLaren, New Zealand Formula One racing driver
3: Edgar Baerlin, UK rackets and real tennis champion 1902-1937
7: Edward Morgan Forster, British author (*A Room With A View, Howard's End, A Passage To India*, etc) *(see Came & Went pages)*
11: Alexander Kerenski, Russian politician, last of pre-communist leaders
21: Ahmed Sukarno, President of Indonesia 1945-67

JUNE 19

Soviets Celebrate Soyuz Space Record

Soviet space scientists were jubilant today as they watched the safe return to central Russia of *Soyuz 9*, the latest craft to push back the boundaries of skill and endurance needed if the USSR was ever to succeed in its bid to put a man on the moon.

Soyuz 9's cosmonauts had displayed both during their 17 days in orbit around the earth - the longest any human had stayed in space. Their experience was bound to provide the Soviet team with invaluable technical and physical data on the stresses space travel puts on the bodies of those who would reach for the stars.

JUNE 22

Methodists Say 'Yes' To Women Ministers

An historic moment for the Methodist Church today when it was announced that a recent poll of worshiping members provided an overwhelming majority in favour of women being allowed to become full ministers. The decision would be ratified at the annual Methodist Conference, which began in Manchester a few days later.

The move was intended to inject much needed vitality into a Methodist movement which had seen membership in Britain alone drop by 11 per cent during the past 10 years, and the number of ministers decrease by almost 300 to only 3,149.

The new women ministers were to have equal pay and enjoy the same status as male ministers in every respect.

JUNE 7

'The Who' Take 'Tommy' To The Met

Usually stuffed to the roof with dinner suits and posh frocks, New York's Metropolitan Opera House played host to a less sedate and far more colourful capacity crowd tonight when British rock band The Who performed their new rock opera *Tommy*.

In an auditorium more accustomed to the works of Verdi, Puccini, Mozart or Bizet, the four London rockers treated a rapt and enthusiastic audience to lead guitarist Pete Townsend's story of a brutalized deaf, dumb and blind boy who finds salvation, fame and fortune as a pin-ball champion. La Traviata it wasn't. A triumph it most certainly was!

Jacklin Ends 50-Year Wait For British US Open Win

IT TOOK 50 LONG YEARS, but the US Open Championship trophy - and winnings of £12,500 ($30,000) - was finally presented once more to a British golfer today when Tony Jacklin (pictured) ended four gruelling rounds of play to join immortals Bobby Jones and Ben Hogan as the only men to have won the British and US Opens within the same 12 months.

The last time a British player won the event, it was the 57 year old Ted Ray in 1920. Then the event was held at Inverness, Ohio and he won by a single stroke. This year's Open was staged at the Hazeltine National golf course in Minneapolis, where the 25 year old Lincolnshire-born Jacklin finished victor by seven strokes to beat a field which included Americans Jack Nicklaus and Arnold Palmer, South African Gary Player and windy conditions which saw the better-fancied locals simply fade and die.

The only golfer in the tournament to finish all four rounds under par, Jacklin flew back to London with his wife and baby son - and that much-coveted trophy.

JUNE

RINDT DIES, BUT STILL HAILED AS CHAMPION

There is little doubt that Jochen Rindt, the Austrian racing driver who dominated the 1970 Formula One racing season with runaway victories in the Monaco, Dutch, French, British and German Grands Prix, would have become one of the all-time greats if he had not been killed in practice for the Italian Grand Prix in September.

As it was, he had already done enough to be the only man ever to win the world championship posthumously, and enter the record books as a formidable racer who'd amassed 109 points from 60 starts.

Orphaned during the war at only 15 months and raised by his grandparents, Rindt established his early reputation on the European circuit and racked up nine Formula Two wins with Brabham in 1967. But it wasn't until he joined Lotus in 1969 that he found himself behind the wheel of a truly competitive Formula One machine.

That season saw only one victory - the US Grand Prix - but his achievements this year marked him as special, and a man who would be especially missed by fans who thrilled at his bravery and immense skill.

The 1970 season also witnessed the tragic loss of Bruce McLaren, the New Zealand ace whose name was destined to live on as a championship marque. He died in June, at Goodwood, where he was testing a sports car prototype.

Graham Hill came close to death in the US Grand Prix at Watkins Glen, and few believed he'd be capable of racing again in 1970. They hadn't reckoned for Hill's dogged determination to carry on. He was back in action for the South African race, but had to be lifted in and out of the cockpit!

SEMI-FINAL BATTLE LEAVES ITALY UNABLE TO HANDLE BRILLIANT BRAZIL

No-one disputed Brazil's right to take the Jules Rimet Trophy home as winners of the 1970 World Cup. Their 4-1 thrashing of Italy in the Azteca Stadium, Mexico City was a comprehensive display of superb team play. But the game of the tournament had been played four days earlier, and that undoubtedly left Italy physically drained and so relatively easy prey for Pelé, Gerson, Jairzinho and Carlos Alberto, Brazil's goal-scorers.

The classic was Italy's semi-final game against West Germany, who'd beaten England 3-2 in extra time three days earlier. They faced another two-hour battle in the Mexican sun when the game was tied 1-1 after 90 minutes.

Extra time was a thriller, with Germany at first leading 2-1, Italy levelling and then leading 3-2, Müller equalling the scoring one more with his 10th goal of the tournament, and Rivera putting in what was to prove the decider straight from the re-start. Six goals in 21 minutes, some of them classics, and all of them deserved.

COLTS AND COWBOYS MEET AS NFC AND AFC MERGE

American Football changed forever, and for the better, this year as the game's two organizing bodies, the AFC and the NFC, finally agreed to merge and give gridiron fans a better structured annual competition and a clear championship battle to climax the season.

New television deals also provided armchair supporters with a feast of options, with CBS buying the rights to NFC games and NBC acquiring AFC fixtures.

The Baltimore Colts emerged as AFC champions when they beat the Oakland Raiders 27-17 in their decider, while the Dallas Cowboys took the NFC title in a season notable for coach Tom Landry's interchanging use of two quarterbacks, Craig Morton and Roger Staubach.

More than 79,000 people were at Miami's Orange Bowl to see the two slug it out for the ultimate championship - a tight game settled in the last quarter when Baltimore linebacker Mike Curtis intercepted a Craig Morton pass to give his place-kicker, Jim O'Brien, a 32-yard field goal chance with only five seconds on the clock. O'Brien slotted it home, and the Colts celebrated a well-earned 16-13 victory.

Jochen Rindt and wife celebrate his dramatic British Grand Prix win

IRA Snipers Fire On British Troops In Belfast Riots

BRITISH TROOPS TODAY confirmed that they have begun facing a new and deadly enemy - the rooftop sniper - during three days of battles with Republicans in the streets of Belfast. Three civilians, including one said to be a sniper, were reported killed during the violence, with 10 soldiers wounded.

As bombs exploded throughout Belfast, British commanders placed 50 streets in the mostly-Catholic area around the Falls Road under curfew, attempting to enforce it with an army helicopter which circled low over the district using a loudspeaker system to warn people that they'd be arrested if they stayed on the streets.

At the height of the most recent violence, which began when a police raid in the Falls Road area discovered an arms store which included a sub-machine gun, a rifle, 15 pistols and ammunition, more than 1,500 British soldiers found themselves involved in running gun battles with IRA snipers while coming under attack from gangs of youths hurling petrol bombs, stones and other missiles, including iron bars. The troops were called in when a crowd which had gathered near the house which had been raided refused to disperse. Tension increased and sparked into violence when CS gas canisters were fired into the crowd. Among buildings worst damaged during the fighting was a newspaper office hit by a bomb thrown from a passing car, while a bomb attack on a Catholic church proved that Protestant extremists were making use of the unrest to stage their own assaults.

Republican opinion would be further outraged on July 13 when, thanks to a massive security operation, the annual Protestant Orange Day parades were able to take place around the province, some of them keeping to traditional routes which brought them within sight and clear sound of Republican districts which had been sealed off for the occasion.

Court Beats King In Wimbledon Battle

In a thrilling climax to the Wimbledon tennis tournament today, the main thrills were delivered by the Ladies' Singles finalists, Australia's Margaret Court and three-times past champion, American ace Billie-Jean King, who was hotly favoured to regain the title she lost last year to Britain's Ann Jones.

In the event, it was Miss Court who emerged victorious, but only after she and Mrs King (the former Billie-Jean Moffitt) thrilled the Centre Court crowd with the longest-ever women's final to produce a score-line which read: 14-12, 11-9.

As had become almost routine in recent years, the Men's Singles was an all-Australian affair which saw last year's loser, John Newcombe (beaten then fellow Aussie Rod Laver), overcome his countryman Ken Rosewall in a titanic tussle which ended 5-7, 6-3, 6-2, 3-6, 6-1.

UK TOP 10 SINGLES

1: In The Summertime
- Mungo Jerry
2: All Right Now
- Free
3: All Around The Bend
- Creedence Clearwater Revival
4: It's All In The Game
- The Four Tops
5: Groovin' With Mr Bloe
- Mr Bloe
6: Cottonfields
- The Beach Boys
7: Sally
- Gerry Monroe
8: Goodbye Sam, Hello Samantha
- Cliff Richard
9: Love Of The Common People
- Nicky Thomas
10: Lola
- The Kinks

Troops On Standby As British Dockers Walk Out

British troops were put on standby today as Prime Minister Edward Heath declared a state of emergency in an attempt to break the national dock strike called by union bosses locked in a bitter pay dispute. The troops could be called in to move freight if the strike dragged on.

The Prime Minister had ordered a full independent inquiry into seamen's pay, but yesterday's decision by union members, to fight for a basic minimum wage of £20 ($45) a week with a full national walk-out, gave him little option.

While food manufacturers warned against panic buying, British industry chiefs stated their fears that the strike could damage international trade. In the event, predictions of a six-week stoppage proved unfounded when, on July 29, dockers accepted an increased pay offer and voted to return to work.

JULY 20

Macleod Death Stuns Heath's New Government

THE NEW CONSERVATIVE government of Edward Heath was shaken and saddened tonight at the death, following a heart attack, of Iain Macleod, the 56 year old appointed Chancellor of the Exchequer only four weeks ago. Besides leaving a huge gap in the new government's ranks, Macleod's death robbed the Conservative left-wing of one of its most able champions and the party as a whole of one of its finest public speakers, ideas men and shrewdest tacticians.

Iain Macleod, who died at his official residence in Downing Street, suffered constant pain from spinal trouble and arthritis, both legacies of injuries he'd received in the war. Despite these handicaps he was a tireless worker and had emerged as one of Mr Heath's most able aides during the Conservative Party's outstanding election campaign.

Forced into a major Cabinet shuffle, Mr Heath appointed Anthony Barber, the Conservative Party chairman who actually managed that campaign, as Iain Macleod's successor.

Forced to carry out his own shuffle following Labour's defeat in the polls, Harold Wilson had gained a new Deputy Leader on July 8 with the appointment of the Welsh-born MP, Roy Jenkins.

JULY 15

Woman Given Nuclear-Driven Pacemaker

An un-named British woman received the most innovative product of atomic research today when surgeons at London's National Heart Hospital gave her a nuclear battery-powered pacemaker designed by scientists working at Britain's atomic energy centre in Harwell, Berkshire.

Powered by plutonium in a capsule sealed into a tiny steel cylinder, the pacemaker was designed to ensure the woman's heart rate maintains a steady 70 beats per minute, and would run for 'at least' ten years.

Concern that the plutonium could leak was allayed by Harwell physicist Dr MJ Poole, who said there was no radioactivity produced when intense heat or a two-ton weight was applied to the capsule. There was therefore no risk if a patient was accidentally burned, or cremated.

Salazar, Dictator Of Portugal, Dies

Antonio de Oliveira Salazar, unquestioned dictator of Portugal from 1932 until a stroke forced his retirement two years ago, died today at the age of 81. A life-long bachelor, he was survived by his two adopted daughters.

The son of a farmer, Salazar emerged as a national figure in 1928 when the leaders of a military coup appointed him Finance Minister in their new government. Given the task of trying to restore Portugal's economy after a century of deficits, he resigned when his initial advice was not taken, but returned two years later under his own terms and produced a budget surplus in his first year back. Appointed Prime Minister, Salazar initiated changes which gave him unparalleled powers and enabled him to steer Portugal through the next 50 years with unquestioned authority.

More Damages For Thalidomide Victims

As predicted in March, when the first High Court lawsuit by Thalidomide victims against the Distillers (Biochemicals) Company ended in victory for them and their families, a precedent had been set to help the arguments of those who brought future actions in Britain and Germany. In London today, a second British trial ended with damages totalling £485,000 ($1,200,000) being awarded to the 28 children whose families had sued Distillers.

Oh! Calcutta! Sex Revue Fails To Turn Critics On

Failing to deliver what its pre-publicity and teasing posters promised - at least to the critics given the task of reviewing it - the uninhibited sex revue *Oh! Calcutta!* opened at London's Roundhouse tonight to give its fashionable, celebrity-rich first night audience a series of sketches, tableaux and dance routines about orgies, lesbians and underwear fetishism.

Devised and directed by theatre critic and TV arts reviewer Kenneth Tynan, *Oh! Calcutta!* did include two dances performed by completely naked men and women. For the rest, which was performed in revealing body stockings, the skimpiest of undies or merely topless, the critics agreed the show was a bit, well, limp. Destined to become a long-running West End attraction and enjoy successful productions in New York and Paris, *Oh! Calcutta!* would confound the opinion of one reviewer who wrote 'It is a mistake to promise more than you can perform, in sex and even more in comedy.'

Nixon Forced To Retract 'Manson Guilty' Goof

PRESIDENT NIXON - himself a lawyer who should have known better - was tonight forced to retract an unguarded statement that Charles Manson (pictured), currently on trial in California charged with the murder of actress Sharon Tate, who was pregnant, and four others last August, was 'guilty, directly or indirectly of eight murders without reason.'

The remarks, made by the President at a press conference and translated into front page news across the United States, were seized on by Manson in a Los Angeles court today. Grinning gleefully, the hippy cult leader waved a newspaper at jurors, showing them the 'Nixon Declares Manson Guilty' headline.

Ordering court officials to seize the paper, the trial judge warned the jury that they should not be swayed by what they had seen. It's not likely the headline would have changed their eventual verdict - the sheer weight of evidence against Manson and his drug-drenched, orgiastic and brutal followers was overwhelming enough.

But Nixon's indiscretion could not go unchallenged. Forced to defend his remarks, the President first tried to clarify them. When this led him into even deeper legal waters, he decided to eat humble pie and retract them altogether.

For the record, Manson and three co-defendants were convicted of the Tate murders on January 25, 1971. Although the prosecution pressed for the death penalty - Manson was also found guilty of complicity in the murders of a Los Angeles couple, the LaBiancas - he would be sentenced to life without parole, a sentence confirmed despite a number of subsequent appeals.

AUGUST 24

Radioactive Leak Forces Windscale Shut-Down

British opponents of atomic energy had their case against the Windscale nuclear power station strengthened today when part of the plant was sealed off following a radioactive leak.

Situated on the coast of Cumberland, Windscale first became the target of a close-down campaign in 1957 when a severe fire forced the permanent shutdown of one of the plant's uranium piles and led to an admitted release of radioactive material into the Irish Sea and the surrounding countryside.

Although officials denied anyone in the area was ever at risk - claims they continued to make - thousands of gallons of admittedly contaminated milk were ordered to be poured into drains and out to sea following that incident.

AUGUST 20

Colombian Court Clears Captain Bobby Moore

There were a few celebratory bottles of champagne popped open in the home of England soccer skipper Bobby Moore tonight as he threw a party to celebrate the long-awaited news from Bogotá, capital of Colombia, the South American country he had sworn never to visit again.

Moore had been waiting three months for three judges to pronounce him innocent of charges laid against him by the owner of an hotel jewellery shop. They decided he was not guilty of stealing an emerald bracelet from the shop - something the star had consistently said all along.

AUGUST 31

Range Rover A Motor Show Smash

Undoubted hit of the British Motor Show held this month at London's Earl's Court exhibition centre, the Rover company's new four-wheel drive Range Rover grabbed all the headlines as thousands of visitors headed for a closer look at what everyone agreed was a pretty nifty machine. Packing a V8 engine - and a suitably-hefty £2,000 ($4,500) price tag - the Range Rover turned out to be a cross between the legendary Land Rover and a very upmarket saloon, with all the rugged cross-country qualities of the former, and all the benefits of the latter.

ARRIVALS

Born this month:

17: Jim Courier, US tennis ace, Davis Cup team member

31: Debbie Gibson (Deborah Ann Gibson), US pop singer (*Shake Your Love, Only In My Dreams, We Could Be Together,* etc)

AUGUST 26

Huge Losses Spell The End For Isle Of Wight Rock

Although it would be hailed as an artistic success by the 600,000 rock fans who flooded through the gates during the three days and nights of the third Isle of Wight Festival, which began tonight, the loss of £90,000 (about $230,000) over the weekend would lead the promoters to announce they would not stage any future events.

They had laid out almost £500,000 to create an all-star line-up which included Jimi Hendrix, The Doors, Joni Mitchell, The Who, Donovan, jazz trumpeter Miles Davis, Ten Years After, Joan Baez and Chicago (pictured). As usual, however, the large number of festival-goers who managed to get into the open air site without paying meant there was an inevitable and sizeable shortfall in vital box office receipts.

British Rail was happy, though. All of the 600,000 who travelled to the Isle of Wight for the Bank Holiday weekend had to use its ferries to get there. And they didn't get away without paying for that!

New Non-Sectarian Party Formed In Ulster

NORTHERN IRISH PEOPLE desperate for a political party which did not follow rigid sectarian lines, were given fresh hope today with the formation of the Social and Democratic Labour Party (SDLP), a group dedicated to achieving vital electoral and legal reforms in an increasingly polarized province.

To be led by Gerry Fitt, a Member of Parliament in Westminster and the Northern Ireland Assembly at Stormont, the SDLP joined the recently-formed Alliance Party as a fresh source of non-sectarian opposition to an Ulster government reeling from crisis to crisis, its hard-line maintenance of the Unionist philosophy making it unwilling, or unable, to reach a compromise with those seeking a solution to Ulster's unionist-republican divide.

The SDLP came into being as Northern Ireland experienced a fresh escalation in civil disturbances dominated by the introduction of rubber bullets to the wide range of weapons already used against rioters by British troops. First fired in Belfast on August 2, they would be employed again - along with CS gas - in Londonderry's Catholic enclave, Bogside, on August 12.

Rover's Return Regulars Celebrate 1000th Opening

The doors of The Rover's Return, arguably Britain's best-known pub, opened for the 1000th time tonight as *Coronation Street*, the twice-weekly soap which has become the country's top-rated TV show celebrated a new landmark in its remarkable success story. First broadcast in 1960 and intended to be a 13-week series, *Coronation Street* was such an overwhelming hit, Granada TV executives decided to continue its run. Since then, this endless saga of working-class folk in a glum northern street had made keeping up with characters like Ena Sharples, Minnie Caldwell, Len Fairclough, Elsie Tanner, Ken Barlow and Annie Walker, the indomitable Rover's Return landlady, an unmissable part of Monday and Wednesday evenings for millions of devoted fans.

Queen And Harper's To Merge

In what may be proof of changing times and a clear sign that the Swinging Sixties are well and truly over, the publishers of top society fashion and lifestyle magazines *Queen* and *Harper's Bazaar* today announced that the two were to merge. Once found jostling for coffee table space with *Vogue* and *The Field* in the homes of all ladies of note, taste and breeding, the two up-market glossies had witnessed a slump in both their sales and influence.

The combined magazine would be called *Harper's*, with a much smaller and *Queen* to maintain the other's presence.

Jackson 5 Have 10 Million Reasons To Smile

Like almost every 'overnight sensation' that ever shot to stardom from nowhere, The Jackson 5 were, in fact, the result of quite a few road miles and an awful lot of grooming before they were launched onto the big stage. In their case, the road miles had been clocked up under the tutelage of their aggressively ambitious father, Joe Jackson, while the grooming had been carried out by America's most successful hit factory, Detroit's Motown Records.

Born and raised in Gary, Indiana, the group Motown launched at the end of 1969 with *I Want You Back* consisted of the brothers Michael (aged only 12), Jermaine (16), Jackie (19), Marlon (23) and Tito (27). Naturally, the focus was firmly on the dynamic and precocious talents of Michael, though the group's non-stop live show proved that all the Jacksons were exceptionally-gifted singers, dancers and musicians.

Initially discovered by Motown star Gladys Knight in 1968, but launched under the sponsorship of Diana Ross, The Jackson 5 were originally promoted to rival the teenybop whimsy of white acts like The Osmonds and The Partridge Family. Instantly successful, The Jackson 5 would rack up 1970 million-sellers with *ABC, The Love You Save* and *I'll Be There* and end the year with total world sales of more than 10 million!

The hits would keep on coming until Michael's departure for a solo career in 1972 meant a change of name for the group to The Jacksons, and an eventual re-writing of pop music history by the youngest brother. Jermaine Jackson would enjoy his share of solo stardom in the 1980s, while baby sister Janet (only three years old when the brothers made their national début!) emerged as a major star in 1986.

Overnight sensations, indeed!

NEED A HIT?
CALL BURROWS AND DANTE!

The history of popular music is full of examples of unsung heroes and heroines, whether it's session musicians whose contributions add a distinctive something to a record which everyone accepts made the difference between it being a hit and an absolute smash, or singers whose uncredited presence helped lift a named lead singer's performance from the mundane to the sublime.

Two of the latter came into their own on both sides of the Atlantic in 1969 and 1970 as producers with hit songs but no artists hit on the relatively simple idea of using the best singers they knew to make those hits and merely attach a fictitious group name to the end result. With enough radio airplay, the non-existent group needn't appear in public.

The British singer to gain most from this simple plan was Tony Burrows, an established and busy session singer whose lead vocals were used to create the Brotherhood Of Man (hits this year: *United We Stand* and *Where Are You Going To My Love)*, Edison Lighthouse (*Love Grows Where My Rosemary Goes*) and White Plains (*My Baby Loves Lovin', I've Got You On My Mind* and *Julie Do Ya Love Me*).

In fact, at one point in February this year, Burrows was at No 1 in the UK charts (as Edison Lighthouse, with

Love Grows), No 17 (as White Plains, with *My Baby Loves Lovin'*) and No 20 (as Brotherhood Of Man, with *United We Stand*)!

The American singer to benefit from this mild deception was Ron Dante, who was the featured voice (plus session musicians and singers) for both The Cuff Links and The Archies – in January this year at Nos 4 and 5 respectively in the UK Top 10 with *Tracy* and *Sugar Sugar*.

The Archies, voices of a hit US TV cartoon series, also had a big hit in the States with *Jingle Jangle*, while Ron Dante/The Cuff Links would also score with *When Julie Comes Around*.

S&G CROSS BRIDGE TO SUPERSTARDOM

Although Paul Simon and Art Garfunkel had enjoyed acclaim and fame on the folk-rock circuit in the mid-late 1960s, and broken through to pop success with Simon's new song for the soundtrack of *The Graduate*, in 1968, the duo made the transition to superstardom in February this year when their album *Bridge Over Troubled Water* became the international phenomenon of 1970.

At one stage, Simon and Garfunkel enjoyed the very rare distinction of holding the No 1 spot in the album and singles charts on both sides of the Atlantic, with the album

spending a total of 10 weeks at the top of the US charts and a staggering 41 weeks as Britain's top-selling album.

In 1971, at the Grammy Awards held to honour 1970's releases, *Bridge Over Troubled Water* would be voted Album of The Year, while the title-track single would win as Record of The Year, Song Of The Year, Best Contemporary Song, Best Arrangement Accompanying Vocalists and Best Engineered Record.

Then they broke up!

The Jackson 5 would end the year with total world sales of more than 10 million!

Palestinians Destroy Hijacked Jets

NINE MASSIVE EXPLOSIONS shattered the calm of the Jordanian desert today as Palestinian terrorists blew up three hijacked airliners in the baking heat of Dawson's Field, an abandoned WWII airstrip built by the RAF.

It was a dramatic end to a saga which began six days ago when PLO guerrillas of the Popular Front for the Liberation of Palestine (PFLP) seized a TWA Boeing 707, a PanAm 747 Jumbo, and a Swissair DC8, all in flight over northern Europe. The PanAm Jumbo was flown to Cairo where, after releasing the passengers and crew, the terrorists blew it up.

A fourth in-flight attack on the same day - this time on an El-Al Boeing 707 - failed when its crew overpowered the two would-be hijackers, killing one and capturing the

other, a woman called Leila Khaled. The pilot landed his plane at London's Heathrow Airport and handed Khaled over to British police.

That failure inspired the PFLP to seize a BOAC VC-10, and it was that plane which the terrorists blew up, along with the Swiss and US aircraft, at Dawson's Field this afternoon. Video footage of the scene showed that only the airliners' tails survived.

Immediate negotiations began to arrange the release of 56 hostages still being held by the PFLP. They had released 255 passengers before destroying the planes, but were holding the others in a secret hide-out. Leila Khaled, the captured hijacker held in London, would prove to be the key to a deal *(see Khaled Swap story)*.

Khaled Swap Gives Hostages Freedom

Leila Khaled, the Palestinian terrorist held in London after she and an accomplice failed in their attempt to hijack an El-Al passenger plane on September 6, was on her way to Beirut tonight aboard an RAF Comet.

Her release - and that of three terrorists held by the Germans, and three others in Swiss custody - was the swap agreed to arrange the release of all the hostages held by Popular Front for the Liberation of Palestine guerrillas since the

Dawson's Field drama on September 12. They, too, are on their way to freedom and a heroes' welcome.

Although the release of the hostages was widely welcomed, there was criticism from some noted commentators. They suggested the deal constituted a dangerous Western climb-down to the Palestinians which could create an unwelcome precedent in future similar hostage situations.

US Open Win Gives Court Second-Only Grand Slam

Australian Margaret Court became only the second woman in history to win the elusive Grand Slam of all four major tennis championships in the same year today when she won the US Open title at Forest Hills, New York.

 Now the undisputed No 1 in the world, the 27 year old ace from New South Wales achieved the remarkable feat by beating America's Rosie Casals over three sets. The only woman to previously complete a Grand Slam of Wimbledon (which Court won in July) and the US, Australian and French Opens, was the immortal Maureen Connolly. 'Little Mo' had her Grand Slam in 1953.

Mary Wilson Publishes Poems From Number 10

Mary Wilson, wife of former Prime Minister Harold Wilson, created chaos in London's Oxford Street today when she agreed to sign copies of her slim volume, Selected Poems , to celebrate its publication. Huge lines of

purchasers formed along the pavements of one of the world's busiest thoroughfares, waiting to buy the instant best-seller and have the author add her autograph.

 Mrs Wilson, who was accompanied by her husband (who kept firmly in

the background with his famous pipe constantly lit), admitted that the excitement of seeing her poems in print didn't match the excitement of living at 10 Downing Street, where some of her verses were written.

UK TOP 10 SINGLES

1: The Tears Of A Clown
- Smokey Robinson & The Miracles
2: The Wonder Of You
- Elvis Presley
3: Give Me Just A Little More Time
- Chairmen Of The Board
4: Mama Told Me Not To Come
- Three Dog Night
5: Band Of Gold
- Freda Payne
6: Make It With You
- Bread
7: Love Is Life
- Hot Chocolate
8: Wild World
- Jimmy Cliff
9: 25 Or 6 To 4
- Chicago
10: Rainbow
- Marmalade

SEPTEMBER 18

Drink And Pills Kill Rock Superstar Jimi

JIMI HENDRIX, THE ROCK GUITARIST who transformed the possibilities of the instrument for a generation of musicians and became one of the world's most popular and explosive entertainers during his relatively brief career, was found dead in London today, the victim of a lethal cocktail of alcohol and sleeping pills. He was 27 years old.

The American-born star's body was found by his German girlfriend, Monika Danneman, in her Notting Hill flat. Ambulance staff called to the scene rushed him to a nearby hospital where doctors declared him dead.

Although Hendrix had a reputation for drug use, a pathologist's report later in the month would confirm he was no junkie - his body showed no needle marks. The report concluded that he had, in fact, died when he inhaled vomit caused by his blend of drink and pills.

Born in Seattle, where his body would be flown for a family funeral, Hendrix was discovered by British musician Chas Chandler in New York, brought to England in 1966 and, with local musicians Noel Redding (on bass) and Mitch Mitchell (drums), formed The Jimi Hendrix Experience. An immediate sensation when launched in 1967, the actually quiet and shy Hendrix used a flamboyant and often controversial psychedelic stage image to sell such hits as *Purple Haze, Stone Free, Hey Joe, Voodoo Chile* and *Foxy Lady* and establish himself as an international sensation.

Known to be unhappy with his current management and career direction, Hendrix had played a disappointing and disjointed show at last month's Isle of Wight Festival. It would prove to be his last public appearance.

Black September For Palestinians

The month which the Palestinians would name Black September came to an uneasy end in Cairo today when King Hussein of Jordan and Palestine Liberation Organization (PLO) leader Yasir Arafat met at an emergency conference brokered by Egypt's President Nasser, and signed a truce agreement to end 10 days of bitter fighting between PLO forces and the Jordanian army.

Although King Hussein - who, like Arafat, wore a symbolic gun belt as he signed the truce - had made some concessions towards Palestinian civilians living in Jordanian refugee camps, the PLO effectively lost all their strongholds in Hussein's kingdom. They had been evicted.

Conflict between the two began when the PLO, supported by the ominous presence of a brigade of Syrian tanks near the Jordanian border, seized control of northern Jordan to threaten the approaches to the capital, Amman. Included in the PLO take-over was Irbid, Jordan's second largest city.

When the Popular Front for the Liberation of Palestine carried out their mass hijack of Western passenger jets, King Hussein decided to act before the war spread. As well as calling on President Nixon for US support - which was given in the form of a full military alert - the King declared a military government, appointing Field Marshal Habis alMajali to head the force ordered to clear out the PLO.

His positions out-flanked and over-run by vastly superior forces, Arafat had only two options: carry on fighting and probably lose everything, or submit to Hussein's eviction notice, find a new home for his guerrillas, and continue his war against Israel from somewhere else.

Nasser Dies At Moment Of Triumph

Only hours after scoring a major personal triumph by persuading King Hussein and Yasir Arafat to sign their truce treaty (see separate story), Egyptian President Gamal Abdel Nasser suffered a massive heart attack and died. He was only 52 years old.

As Arab leaders began to flood Cairo with messages of sympathy and support for his grieving people, it was announced that Nasser's closest friend and most trusted confidant, Anwar Sadat, would succeed him as President.
(*See Came & Went pages*)

OCTOBER 4

Heroin Overdose Claims Rock Singer Janis

AS ROCK FANS BEGAN to recover from the tragic death of Jimi Hendrix in London last month, news broke today that the body of rock singer Janis Joplin - like Hendrix, only 27 years old - had been found in a Hollywood bedroom. Witnesses reported fresh injection marks in her arm and heroin paraphernalia around her body.

A woman who enjoyed a reputation of living her life to the limits expected of a rock star, Joplin was born in Port Arthur, Texas, and began singing blues and folk material while a student at the University of Texas, in Austin. In 1966 she followed the hippie trail to San Francisco, where she became vocalist with the acid-rock band Big Brother And The Holding Company.

Her local fame and popularity became international in 1967 when, like Jimi Hendrix and soul singer Otis Redding, she went for broke with an outstanding, go-for-broke performance at the Monterey Pop Festival. Signed to a management contract with Bob Dylan's mentor, Albert Grossman, Joplin and Big Brother's 1967 début album *Cheap Thrills* sold more than a million copies.

Leaving the group, Joplin scored another hit with her 1969 solo album *I Got Dem Ol' Kozmic Blues Again, Mama* and began to cut a swathe through the world concert and festival circuit with her own Full Tilt Boogie Band. A notoriously heavy drinker, she also began to experiment with the hard drugs which would eventually claim her life.

In the process of recording a new album with Full Tilt when she died, the posthumously released *Pearl* (Joplin's nickname among close friends) would prove an even bigger seller than those she'd made during her short, fast-lived life.

OCTOBER 19

BP Hit Black Gold In North Sea

British Petroleum (BP) today confirmed that one of its exploration teams had made the first major find of oil in the British sector of the North Sea. A test well some 100 miles east of the Scottish port of Aberdeen had hit 'black gold', which was now coming to the surface at the rate of 4,700 barrels a day.

BP was only one of a number of major companies granted government licences to explore what oil experts believed was the most promising area off the Scottish coast. It lay near Norway's Ekofisk oilfield, and BP were hopeful that their find would prove as big as Ekofisk - discovered in June, it was now believed capable of supplying as much as 10 per cent of Britain's total needs.

OCTOBER 16

Anwar Sadat Confirmed As Nasser's Heir

Anwar Sadat was confirmed as the new President of Egypt today when a plebiscite held to approve an Arab Socialist Union central committee recommendation resulted in overwhelming support for one of the late President Nasser's oldest, closest and most trusted friends and political allies.

Millions of weeping Egyptians had filled the streets of Cairo on October 1 as President Nasser's funeral took place, and the 51 year old Sadat - already appointed acting president - was prominent among the official mourners, who included leading Arab world figures and representatives of many Western nations.

Considered to be a moderate, and certainly less flamboyant than the man he succeeds, Sadat helped Nasser and a group of young officers plan the coup which overthrew King Farouk in 1952. An experienced politician, he is expected to take a more conciliatory line in regional politics.

OCTOBER 23

Irish Court Clears Haughey Of Gun-Running

THE IRISH HIGH COURT exploded into a roar of cheers and applause today as Charles Haughey, the former Finance Minister in Prime Minister Jack Lynch's cabinet, was acquitted - along with four co-defendants - of charges alleging the illegal importing of arms. Another former minister, Neil Blaney, had been cleared of the same charges in July. It was an open secret that the Irish authorities believed that Haughey, a fervent and openly anti-British nationalist, had intended the arms to go to IRA guerrillas locked in an increasingly bloody conflict in Ulster.

For his part, Haughey successfully persuaded the Dublin court that he and his colleagues had become innocently embroiled in an officially-sanctioned undercover intelligence operation for the Irish Army. This had gone wrong when police discovered the arms cache, and he was merely a sacrificial lamb in a cover-up exercise.

Told of Haughey's acquittal while in New York, PM Jack Lynch said he had done what he believed to be his duty when he dismissed Haughey from office. Aware that the reputation of his government would suffer from the Haughey affair, Mr Lynch would not be drawn into speculation on his erstwhile colleague's political future.

After a relatively short period of reflection, Charles Haughey would bounce back and, during the 1980s, would serve as Eire's Prime Minister on three occasions, proving a formidable and hard-nosed negotiator against Margaret Thatcher as the Ulster problem continued to remain unresolved.

OCTOBER 16

Trudeau Sends Troops To Subdue Quebec Rebels

Canadian Prime Minister Pierre Trudeau moved decisively against Quebec separatists and the Quebec Liberation Front (FLQ) terrorist group today when he declared the province to be in 'a state of insurrection', outlawed the FLQ and ordered 1,500 paratroopers to take over strategic points in and around Montreal, the French-Canadian capital.

Trudeau's actions followed two FLQ outrages - the kidnapping of British diplomat James Cross on October 5, and that of Pierre Laporte, Quebec's Labour and Immigration Minister, five days later.

With negotiations for the men's release stalled, Trudeau decided to dictate the pace. During police raids on FLQ offices, 250 supporters were arrested, including Robert Lemieux, the FLQ's chief negotiator.

While James Cross would finally be released in December, on October 18 the dead body of Pierre Laporte was discovered in an abandoned car.

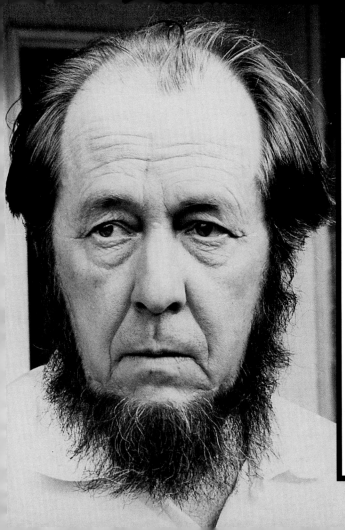

Stubborn Solzhenitsyn: 'I Will Accept Nobel Prize'

Soviet author Alexander Solzhenitsyn - banned for his strong opposition to the state censorship of literature - became the centre of a major literary row in Moscow today when he confirmed that he intended to travel to Stockholm in December to accept the Nobel Prize for Literature he'd won for works such as The First Circle and The Cancer Ward. A survivor of Stalin's notorious death camps, Solzhenitsyn drew heavily on his horrific experiences to create his most notable books, inevitably leading to them being banned in Russia. The official Writers' Union - which expelled him last year - was expected to pressure Solzhenitsyn into rejecting the Nobel Prize, as it did successfully with Boris Pasternak, author of Dr Zhivago, in 1958.

OCT

President Nasser (centre) with King Hussein (right) and Yasir Arafat (left).

SEPT 28

NASSER- THE BROKEN -HEARTED DREAMER

A fervent believer in Arab nationalism, Abdul Gamal Nasser was a member of the Egyptian military junta which seized power and forced the abdication of King Farouk in 1952. A young Colonel at the time of the coup, he succeeded the junta's leader, General Neguib, as Prime Minister in 1954 before becoming President later that year.

His nationalization of the Suez Canal triggered the British-French invasion of Egypt in 1956. Their humiliating retreat when the US refused to back the action, raised Nasser's prestige in the Arab world, enabling him to realize his dream of a United Arab Republic - effectively a coalition with Syria - in 1958.

Forced by left-wing opinion to take an increasingly hostile stance against Israel, in 1967 Nasser suffered the humiliation of overwhelming defeat in the Six-Day War. Persuaded to withdraw his resignation as President, he managed to maintain close links with Moscow while generally improving Egypt's relationship with the United States - a move which was especially attacked by Yasir Arafat's PLO and Libya's Colonel Gaddafi.

The inability of rival Arab states to unite in peace would prove a perpetual source of grief for Nasser, and it was said that this year's expulsion from Jordan of the PLO was the final, fatal blow for a man who was ruled by his heart. When that heart gave in today, Nasser was only 52 years old.

JUNE 8
EM FORSTER - A MAN WITH A VIEW

It's difficult to imagine how a novelist as gifted and successful as Edward Morgan Forster, who died today at the age of 91, could have simply stopped writing fiction at the age of 45 and devoted the rest of his life to writing about writing in books, essays and literary reviews. But he did.

Fortunately, before he stopped creating timeless and exquisitely-observed characters and situations, EM Forster left the legacy of such classics as *A Room With A View, Howard's End, A Passage To India* and *Maurice* - all of which now live on to a far wider audience as the inspiration for superb films.

After graduating from King's College, Cambridge in 1897, Forster travelled extensively around the Mediterranean, an experience which inspired him to write his first novel, *Where Angels Fear To Tread,* in 1905.

A period in India as private secretary to a maharajah would result in his 1924 masterpiece, *A Passage To India,* but it was his homosexuality - naturally hidden from the world at large - which would inspire his novel Maurice, and lead to it not being published until 1971.

Always concerned with the liberty of the individual, in 1934 Forster became the first President of Britain's National Council for Civil Liberties.

JULY 7
SIR ALLEN LANE - THE SIXPENNY MILLIONAIRE

The idea of publishing books with thin paper covers was hardly new in 1936 - a number of American, British and European companies were already churning out the aptly-named pulp fiction that way. But it was Allen Lane who realized that 'good' books would reach a far wider audience if they were made available in such a format. And that is how Penguin Books was born.

Justly rewarded with a knighthood in 1952, Sir Allen Lane began his career in publishing with *The Bodley Head,* but it was when his conviction that there was a future in publishing quality paperbacks was met with blank stares in that company that he decided to go it alone.

The immediate and resounding success of Penguin books (which were costed at an easily-affordable sixpence each), especially when Sir Allen began publishing cheap editions of copyright-free literary classics by the likes of Shakespeare, Wordsworth and others, meant that his vision was transformed into phenomenal success and a domination of the UK book market.

Expanded to include Puffin (for children's fiction) and Pelican (for non-fiction), the Penguin family simply revolutionized publishing in Britain, Europe and the world.

150,000 Killed As Tidal Wave Hits East Pakistan

A MASSIVE INTERNATIONAL relief and aid programme began in earnest today as the world responded to news that at least 150,000 people were known to have died last week when a massive tidal wave and typhoon swept through East Pakistan, one of the world's most impoverished and densely populated nations.

Britain and American planes arrived in Dhaka, the East Pakistan (now Bangladesh) capital, laden with food, medical supplies, vehicles and helicopters, while the Royal Navy's assault ship Intrepid and repair vessel Triumph were also headed for Dhaka to set up supply and communications centres to help co-ordinate the relief effort. Described by witnesses as being 'as high as a two-storey building', the tidal wave swept away whole villages, killing people and livestock, and completely changing the entire Ganges-Bay of Bengal delta region as it submerged whole islands and created new ones.

Only as the waters began receding was it possible for authorities to see the full extent of the disaster, but it would be some time before a number of outlying areas could be reached. The wave simply washed away roads, while the currents in newly-formed gullies proved too strong for relief boats to get through.

The greatest priority for locals and relief workers would be to locate and bury the thousands of bodies which littered the countryside. As a heatwave hit East Pakistan, the risks of disease among survivors were too awful to contemplate.

UK TOP 10 SINGLES

1: Woodstock
- Matthews' Southern Comfort
2: Patches
- Clarence Carter
3: War
- Edwin Starr
4: Indian Reservation
- Don Fardon
5: Voodoo Chile
- The Jimi Hendrix Experience
6: The Witch
- The Rattles
7: Ruby Tuesday
- Melanie
8: San Bernadino
- Christie
9: Me And My Life
- The Tremeloes
10: Black Night
- Deep Purple

NOVEMBER 27

Gay Lib Stage First London Demo

Already a powerful lobby in the United States, the Gay Liberation Front staged its first public demonstration in London today to protest against prejudice and discrimination in all areas of life, including workplaces, the armed forces, but most of all in public.

Although boasting only 250 British members, some of them sympathetic heterosexuals, Gay Liberation aimed to change public opinion and make it possible for gay men and women to express their affection openly, without shame and without fear of intimidation or arrest.

As one man at the rally said: 'We don't want to be a freak show - we just want to be the same as anybody else, with the same rights.'

NOVEMBER 6

NASA Launches 'Spy In The Sky'

Conspiracy and 'Big Brother is watching you' theorists had a 'Told you so!' field day today when NASA - the US space agency - announced that it had successfully launched America's most sophisticated satellite into orbit. Packed with state-of-the-art surveillance equipment, the newest chunk of metal whirling around in space was said to be able to detect and photograph missile launches anywhere in the world.

Immediately dubbed 'the spy in the sky', the satellite came in for strong condemnation from the Soviet Union, who said its arrival spelled the end of 'innocent' tests of strategic importance.

NOVEMBER 25

Japanese Author Commits Hara-Kiri

Japan was stunned today by the death of best-selling and influential author Yukio Mishima. He committed hara-kiri, the traditional method of suicide using a sword to disembowel oneself and still viewed in some sections of Japanese society as the most honourable way to go.

A noted right-wing traditionalist who had formed a hard-line extremist sect with devoted followers, Mishima took his distaste of what he considered to be the decadence of modern Japan to the limit. After striding into the headquarters of the Defence Ministry in Tokyo to deliver an impassioned appeal for a return to the militarism he believed had made Japan a great nation in the past, Mishima reinforced his point - with the point of his ceremonial sword.

Police Save Pope From Manila Knife-Man

Pope Paul VI escaped injury, or worse, in the Philippine capital, Manila, today when a man wielding a knife was wrestled to the ground by alert security men as he made a lunge at the world leader of the Roman Catholic Church.

Although TV cameras captured the incident - which became almost immediate world headline news when footage was sold to the major networks and press agencies - Pope Paul was apparently unaware that a serious attack had been thwarted as he walked, smiling and blessing those around him, through the biggest crowd Manila had ever witnessed.

On a state visit to the largely Catholic and formerly Spanish-ruled South-East Asian island group, the Pope had also made world headlines only four days earlier, when Vatican Radio announced that he had barred cardinals over the age of 80 from voting in future papal elections.

France Weeps For De Gaulle

THE ORDINARY PEOPLE OF FRANCE today paid tribute to General Charles de Gaulle, World War II leader of the French Army in exile and principal architect of the modern nation re-built from the ruins of that war, when church bells rang out across the country at 3 pm, echoing those which tolled in the church of Colombey-les-Deux-Eglises during the simple family funeral the former President had ordered before his death on November 9.

In accordance with the General's wishes, no members of the government were invited to attend his funeral. Instead, the narrow streets of the little country town to which he'd retired after his resignation last year, were packed with tens of thousands of 'the men and women of France and elsewhere' he had asked 'to do my memory the honour of accompanying my body to the grave.'

That grave would be a simple white marble slab, identical to that of his mentally retarded daughter, Anne, beside whom the General had asked to be buried.

In contrast to the ceremony which a radio commentator described as 'grandiose in its rustic simplicity', a Requiem Mass held at Notre Dame in Paris was the setting for all the pomp and ceremony de Gaulle's former colleagues felt his death was due.

More than 6,000 of the world's great and good filled the cathedral, among them de Gaulle's successor, President Georges Pompidou, US President Richard Nixon, Soviet President Nikolai Podgorny, Britain's Prince Charles, Prime Minister Edward Heath and former PMs Lord Avon and Harold Macmillan, Indian premier Indira Gandhi, Queen Juliana of The Netherlands and the Shah of Iran.

Later, in the evening, hundreds of thousands ignored rain and cold winds to march in silent respect to the Arc de Triomphe, France's permanent memorial to her dead heroes. Observers noted that Paris had witnessed such huge crowds on only two previous occasions - in August 1944, when they celebrated the city's liberation by de Gaulle and his Free French forces, and May 1958, when they gathered to greet the General's election of the Fifth Republic.

On November 13, Place de l'Etoile in Paris was renamed Place Charles de Gaulle.

Britain Reels Under Record Strikes

The first months of Britain's new Conservative government were marred by the loss of more working days through strikes and stoppages than any comparable period since 1926, the year of the General Strike.

According to government figures released today in London, a staggering 8.8 million days had already been lost in 1970, mostly in engineering businesses and trade.

While there had been major disputes involving national newspaper printers, dockers and local authority workers, the bulk of that expensive lost time was caused by a huge number of small stoppages lasting only a matter of hours - but still damaging the British economy and its international trade reputation.

Gomulka Steps Down As Riots Rock Poland

POLAND HAD A NEW leader tonight when Communist Party boss Wladyslaw Gomulka resigned after a week of anti-government riots over rising food prices saw Polish militia opening fire on unarmed workers. His place was taken by Edward Gierek, a 57 year old ex-miner who would promise a two-year price freeze on December 23.

Gomulka's troubles began when protests in the Baltic port of Gdansk against increases in meat and other staple food prices become uncontrollable. Unrest spread and, in the next few days, crowds set fire to the local Communist Party headquarters and looted shops.

At the height of disturbances on December 16, six people were officially reported as having been killed, although a Swedish journalist in the area said he'd been told that 'at least' 300 people, women and children included, had perished in Gdansk.

With riots starting up in other coastal towns, Gomulka ordered militia into the region, giving them freedom to fire on protestors. Faced by an ever-worsening scenario, he decided to quit - 14 years after anti-government riots in Poznan forced the departure of Edward Ochab and Gomulka's arrival was greeted as the dawn of a new, liberal era in modern Polish history.

My Lai GIs Tell Calley Trial: 'We Followed Orders'

With his court martial for the murder of 109 Vietnamese civilians at My Lai in 1968 almost a month old, Lt William Calley (pictured) and his defence team today called the first of their witnesses to rebut US Army prosecution evidence of events the day a patrol led by Calley slaughtered all 567 inhabitants of the village.

Like Calley, all the patrol members who appeared today claimed that they believed that Captain Ernest Medina, their commanding officer and also facing murder charges, had given them orders to kill every living person in My Lai, deep in the heart of a wild area of country known to harbour communist Viet Cong guerrillas.

The My Lai trial would last until March 1971, when Capt Medina would be acquitted. Calley, however, would initially be sentenced to life imprisonment, a penalty substantially reduced, thanks partly to the intervention of President Nixon.

Heath Creates Court To Curb Unions

British MPs tonight voted to establish an Industrial Relations Court with the power to fine trade unions which ignore new procedures aimed at settling industrial disputes without strikes. Introduced by Prime Minister Edward Heath, the legislation came as Britain experienced widespread workplace unrest which had recently included disruption of electricity supplies. Although the Conservatives' Industrial Relations Bill included strike-curbing measures similar to the In Place of Strife plan the Labour government abandoned last year when faced down by the biggest unions, Labour leader Harold Wilson led the opposition against the government Bill. He may have agreed with Mr Heath that Britain was sick of wildcat strikes, but he didn't like the medicine the Prime Minister dished up.

UK TOP 10 SINGLES

1: I Hear You Knocking
- Dave Edmunds
2: When I'm Dead And Gone
- McGuinness Flint
3: Cracklin' Rosie
- Neil Diamond
4: It's Only Make Believe
- Glen Campbell
5: You've Got Me Dangling On A String
- Chairmen Of The Board
6: Ride A White Swan
- T Rex
7: Voodoo Chile
- The Jimi Hendrix Experience
8: I'll Be There
- The Jackson Five
9: Home Lovin' Man
- Andy Williams
10: Indian Reservation
- Don Fardon

DECEMBER 26

Olympic Medallist Lillian Killed By Cancer

LILLIAN BOARD, the outstanding British athlete even the most impartial sports commentators predicted would become one of the world greats, died today after a long fight with cancer. She was only 22 years old.

Lillian's precocious talent first blossomed on the international stage of the 1968 Olympic Games in Mexico City, when she was forced to settle for a silver medal in the 400 metres final, a review of the photo-finish showing that she'd been beaten - just - by French champion Colette Besson.

Switching to 800 metres for the 1969 season, Lillian powered her way to a gold in the European Championships in Athens, and collected a second winner's medal when she anchored Britain's 4X400 relay team. That victory was made sweeter by the fact that the opponent she inched past in the final straight was Colette Besson.

Undergoing treatment in a Bavarian clinic when she died, Lillian Board's courage in her last days moved her friends and fans every bit as much as her athletic brilliance had once thrilled them.

DECEMBER 3

Quebec Terrorists Release British Consul

James Cross, the British consul kidnapped by the Quebec Liberation Front (FLQ) in October and held hostage while the Canadian government of Pierre Trudeau tried to negotiate a face-saving formula for his release, found himself on a plane bound for Havana and freedom today.

With Cross, who would also find his family waiting anxiously when his plane touched down, were Cuban diplomats into whose protective custody the FLQ had released him. Cross would only be completely free once the three FLQ kidnappers who'd held him also reached Havana on a separate flight.

One of the first people to speak to Cross, who was snatched at the same time as the murdered Quebec Minister of Labour, Pierre Laporte, was Canadian premier Trudeau. Clearly delighted, Trudeau told journalists that Cross had said he was in good health and told him: 'The nightmare is over!'

DECEMBER 18

German Thalidomide Victims Awarded £11 Million

In Bonn, the lengthy trial hearing evidence in the lawsuit action taken by hundreds of German families against the German manufacturers of Thalidomide, the morning sickness 'cure' which resulted in thousands of disabled babies in Europe, ended today with an unprecedented award of £11 million ($27m) damages to those so cruelly damaged.

Campaigners who'd fought for justice were obviously delighted. The positive results of two actions against the British distributors had clearly proved the manufacturer's liability, but properly run trust funds would make today's award a source of much-needed income for the rest of the victims' lives.

DECEMBER 10

Solzhenitsyn Accepts His Nobel Prize

Russian author Alexander Solzhenitsyn's decision to accept the 1970 Nobel Prize for Literature, which was formally awarded him in absentia today in Stockholm, set the strong-minded dissident against the full weight of the all-powerful Communist Party - weight which would come down heavily on him within days as he became the subject of public vilification by Pravda, the Party's official newspaper.

On December 17, a Pravda editorial would slam the writer, his work, his decision to accept the capitalist gift, and describe him as 'alien and hostile' to the Soviet people. The publication, in the West, of his masterpiece The Gulag Archipelago - a full description of Stalin's death camps - would lead, in 1974, to Solzhenitsyn being stripped of his Soviet citizenship and expelled into what would be a 20-year exile.

Unlike most Western horoscope systems which group astrological signs into month-long periods based on the influence of 12 constellations, the Chinese believe that those born in the same year of their calendar share common qualities, traits and weaknesses with one of 12 animals - Rat, Ox, Tiger, Rabbit, Dragon, Snake, Horse, Sheep, Monkey, Rooster, Dog or Pig.

They also allocate the general attributes of five natural elements - Earth, Fire, Metal, Water, Wood - and an overall positive or negative aspect to each sign to summarize its qualities.

If you were born between February 17, 1969 and February 5, 1970, you are a Monkey. As this book is devoted to the events of 1970, let's take a look at the sign which governs those born between February 6 that year and January 26, 1971 - The Year of The Dog.

THE DOG
FEBRUARY 6, 1970 - JANUARY 26, 1971
ELEMENT: EARTH   ASPECT: (+)

Dog individuals are the most humanitarian, being givers who are prepared to sacrifice anything in life for those they love. Dogs were born to serve unselfishly, putting the needs of others first and themselves last.

Loyal to those they love, Dogs will always defend any member of their family or friends being attacked by word or deed. Equal rights and seeing justice done are of paramount importance to Dogs, who will always speak out on behalf of the less able.

Inevitably, Dogs' willingness to help can sometimes be misconstrued as interfering nosiness and being too ready to give advice that hasn't been requested.

But it is this essentially idealistic streak in Dogs' nature which makes them genuinely well-meaning people. Indeed, many turn their talents to voluntary or community work and will be tireless in their efforts to right injustice and inequality, and to improve the general lot of the less fortunate in society.

Dogs are solid, steady workers who put consistent effort into whatever they're doing, often to the point of obstinacy. But they rarely take on more than they can reasonably handle.

With their forthright honesty and humanitarianism, Dogs become respected members of society, trusted by all who come to know them. Loyal to friends and superiors, they will always make time to listen to people's problems, and the saying 'A man's best friend is his dog' sums up their dependability, loyalty and their apparent ability to find a kind word to say about everyone.

If Dogs do have a problem, it lies in their finding it hard to adapt to change, and many Dogs prefer to stick it out in the same situation rather than face facts and begin again. This may be because Dogs are innately pessimistic and inclined to expect the worst - a trait which can spoil their happiness. They will make changes if forced to, but tend to remain strongly nostalgic.

Another problem with Dog individuals is their tendency to live with an inherent inner anxiety. Though apparently composed on the surface, they have a deep-down sense of unease. But of all the animals in the Chinese zodiac, Dogs are the most unselfish, caring more about people than they do about money or personal success.

FAMOUS DOGS

Madonna	**HRH Prince William**
singer, dancer, actress	**Michael Jackson**
Mother Teresa	singer, writer, dancer, actor
Nobel Prize-winning nun	**Brigitte Bardot**
Daley Thompson	former sex goddess,
Olympic decathlete	now animal rights
Sylvester Stallone,	campaigner
actor, writer, director	**Ilie Nastase,**
Ralph Nader	Romanian tennis ace
American consumer	**Liza Minelli**
affairs guru	actress, singer, dancer